I0154297

Abraham Lincoln

Humorous and pathetic Tales of Abraham Lincoln

A Collection of Anecdotes and Stories told by and of President Lincoln

Abraham Lincoln

Humorous and pathetic Tales of Abraham Lincoln
A Collection of Anecdotes and Stories told by and of President Lincoln

ISBN/EAN: 9783337136956

Printed in Europe, USA, Canada, Australia, Japan

Cover: Foto ©ninafisch / pixelio.de

More available books at **www.hansebooks.com**

UMOROUS AND PATHETIC TALES OF

ABRAHAM LINCOLN.

A Collection of Anecdotes and Stories Told by and of

PRESIDENT LINCOLN

Many of them Heretofore Unpublished

―――――

THE AD PUBLISHING COMPANY.
CHICAGO, ILL.

PREFACE.

There is no work more important to posterity than perpetuating in literature the lives of great men. Written biography is a valuable acquisition of modern ages and was not known to the ancients. In every period of the world's history, however, the necessity of preserving the records of their great dead has been realized by the people even to the barbarian races and tribes. This fact has been evidenced by the archaeologists in their investigations among the mound builders, and unearthed cities. At buried Memphis monuments of stone were discovered, covered with hieroglyphics telling the stories of men who had achieved honor and glory in their distinctive spheres. In presenting to readers Lincoln's stories, there is a feeling of satisfaction that they will be well received. No man has lived in the history of this country who holds a more sacred place in the minds of the people than Honest Abe Lincoln, as he was familiarly known His steadfastness of purpose, clear discernment, and equity of judgment peculiarly fitted him for the high position of Chief Executive of this nation at a time when the seeds of disunionism were being scattered broadcast throughout the land. Like Moses, who delivered the Children of Israel from bondage, so Abraham Lincoln freed from the coercion of the white master the poor black slave, and kept intact the Union of this glorious Republic. Although Abraham Lincoln possessed many idiosyncrasies, none of them was more marked than his penchant for story telling. There is hardly an instance in even the most serious of his interviews, that the familiar phrase, "That reminds me of a story," was not introduced. In collecting these memoirs of Lincoln we are indebted to the press, to friends, and to J. B. McClure's "Anecdotes of Abraham Lincoln."

CHARACTERISTICS OF MR. LINCOLN.

Secretary Usher, a member of Lincoln's Cabinet, and an old friend of his, gives the following interesting information:

AS A LAWYER.

"Lincoln belonged to the reasoning class of men. He dealt with his own mind and turned things over there, seeking the truth until he established it and it became a conviction. As a lawyer, he never claimed everything for his client. He stated something of both sides of the case. I have known him to say: 'Now, I don't think my client is entitled to the whole of what he claims. In this point or that point he may have been in error. He must rebate something of his claim.' He was also very careful about giving personal offense, and if he had something severe to say, he would turn to his opponent or to the person about to be referred to and say: 'I don't like to use this language,' or, 'I am sorry that I have to be hard on that gentleman;' and, therefore, what he did say was thrice as effective, and very seldom wounded the person attacked. Throughout Mr. Lincoln's life that kind of wisdom attended him, and made him the great and skillful politician he was in handling people. He had a smooth, manly, pleasing voice, and when arguing in court, that voice attracted the jury, and did not tire them, so that they followed his argument throughout. He was not a graceful man. He would lean on the back of a chair, or put the chair behind him, or stand hipshotten, or with arms akimbo, but yet there was a pleasure in listening to him, because he seemed so unmercenary.

HIS AMBITION.

"I do not think Lincoln was ambitious at all. It seems to me that his object in life was no greater than to make a living for his family. The dream of avarice never crossed him. He took no initial steps to reach the Presidency or the Senate, and was rather pushed forward, than a volunteer. I can't recall in those days when he attended court that he ever spoke about himself or took any satisfaction in victory over an adversary, or repeated any good thing he had done or said. As a partisan he always reasoned for the good of the party, and not concerning his own advancement. Consequently, when the people had made up their minds that there was talent in him, of a remarkable kind, they came to his assistance with a spontaneity and vehemence that was electrical. He reaped the great reward of unselfishness as few men have ever done.

HIS NATURE.

"I can recall a certain incident that illustrates Lincoln's nature. Somewhere near the town of Parris there was a Whig population with strong prejudices in favor of protecting slavery. These people liked Lincoln, and believed in him, and saw with pain that he was becoming a Radical. They came to him during court and said: 'We want you to come up and talk to us. We don't want to quarrel with you, and will hear all you have to say; but something must be wrong when as fair a man as you is drifting over to

4

Abolitionism.' 'Very well,' said Mr. Lincoln, 'I will come up on such a day and give you my views.' Lincoln went on that day, and made a temperate, sweet-toothed, cordial address on the issues of the day. He said: 'My friends, I perceive you will not agree with me but that ought to make no difference in our relations with each other. You hear me, as you always have, with kindness, and I shall respect your views, as I hope you will mine.' They heard Lincoln through, and dismissed him with respect, but did not agree with him. There was another person up there by the name of Stephens, who was lame, and he undertook to emphasize Lincoln's views, and put his foot on it. A certain doctor, of Southern origin, interrupted Stephens, and said he would thrash him. Stephens turned around and replied, 'Well, doctor, you can thrash me, or do anything of a violent sort to me, if you don't give any of your pills.' Lincoln used to tell this with a good deal of delight. You see, in those days the settlers in Illinois would live in the edges of the timber, which grew in spots and patches, and left naked prairie between the groves. It was at such a place that Lincoln made that speech on the slavery question.

ABRAHAM AND THE LADIES.

"He was almost wholly possessed with a sense of duty and responsibility. He was not shy in the company of ladies, but I don't think he thought anything about them until they came before him as guests and callers. Some of the women gave him a good deal of trouble. Some of his wife's people were Southerners, and public attacks were made on them; as, for instance, it was said that one of them had gone through the lines with a pass from Mr. Lincoln, and taken a quantity of medicine, etc. I remember that an old partner in law of mine brought his wife to Washington, and they wanted to see Mr. Lincoln. There was a great crowd awaiting around his door, but the doorkeeper admitted us at once, and Mr. Lincoln came forward with both hands extended and shook the lady's hand, rather divining that she was the wife of my partner. He told a little anecdote or two, and said some quaint things, and when the lady came out, she said to me: 'Why, I don't think that he is an ugly man at all.' He was almost a father to his wife. He seemed to be possessed of the notion that she was under his protection, and that he must look out for her like a willful child.

LINCOLN'S TEMPER.

I remember one event showing Lincoln's temper. He had issued a proclamation stating that when one-tenth of the voters of a Congressional district, or a part of a State, resumed their position in the Union, and elected a member of Congress, they should be recognized as much as the whole constituency. Chase remarked: 'Instead of saying voters, I suggest that you put in citizens!' I saw in a minute what Chase was driving at. This question had arisen, as to who were citizens, and Mr. Bates, the Attorney General, had pronounced negroes to be citizens. The law of the administration, therefore, was, that negroes were included in citizenship. As I walked away from the Cabinet that day Chase was at my side, and he said: 'Mr. Usher, we must stick to it that citizens, and not voters, be named in that proclamation.' I turned about when we had got to the Treasury, and walked back on the plank which at that time led to the White House, and I told Lincoln that Chase was very pertniacious about the word citizens instead of voters. 'Yes,' said Lincoln, "Chase thinks that the negroes, as citizens, will all vote to make him President.'

HIS SADNESS.

"Lincoln was, in his fixed quality, a man of sadness. If he were looking out a window when alone, and you happened to be passing by and caught his eye, you would generally see in it an expression of distress.

"He was one of the greatest men who ever lived. It has now been many years since I was in his Cabinet, and some of the things which happened there have been forgotten, and the whole of it is rather dreamy. But Lincoln's extraordinary personality is still one of the most distinct things in my memory. He was as wise as a serpent. He had the skill of the greatest statesman in the world. Everything he handled came to success. Nobody took up his work and brought it to the same perfection.

HIS KINDNESS.

"Lincoln had more patience than anybody around him. Sometimes, when we were considering a thing of importance in the Cabinet, his little son would push open the door and come in with a drum and beat it up and down the room, giving us all a certain amount of misery. Mr. Lincoln, however, never ordered the boy to be taken out, but would say: 'My son, don't you think you can make a little less noise?' That Thaddeus was a stubborn little chap. We could not make up with him when he got offended. Robert was as well-behaved a young man as I have ever seen. He went to Hartford and graduated, and we entertained high respect for him.

LINCOLN AND SEWARD.

"I think that Lincoln had a real fondness and admiration for Seward. There was no suspicion or rivalry whatever, between them. Seward supported Lincoln in every position or scruple that he had. My impression is, that those two men were as cordial and intimate as any two persons of such prominence could be.

"After Caleb Smith, of Indiana, was made a member of the Cabinet, he desired me to be his Assistant Secretary. Mr. Smith was nominated District Judge of the United States in the course of time, and then Mr. Lincoln promoted me at Smith's request. I was in the Cabinet somewhat more than two years, and a part of the time was under Mr. Johnson. That Cabinet was very ill-assorted. My predecessor, Judge Smith, was a kind man, but without much discrimination as to his followers. There hardly was ever such a thing as a regular Cabinet meeting in the sense of form. Under Johnson and under Grant, I have seen a table with chairs placed in regular order around it, as if for Cabinet council. Nothing of that kind ever occurred in Mr. Lincoln's Cabinet. Seward would come in and lie down on a settee. Stanton hardly ever stayed more than five or ten minutes. Sometimes Seward would tell the President the outline of some paper he was writing on a State matter Lincoln generally stood up and walked about. In fact, every member of that Cabinet ran his own Department in his own way. I don't suppose that such a historic period was ever so simply operated from the

8

center of powers. Lincoln trusted all his subordinates and they worked out their own performances. I regard Seward, as on the whole the strong man of the Cabinet, the counsel of the President.

LINCOLN AND MRS. FREMONT.

"Well, there was the case of John Fremont. He had made up his mind to run a little enterprise of his own. When he got into Missouri he soon quarreled with Frank Blair, and Montgomery Blair started on to St. Louis. Meantime Mrs. Fremont came East, passing Blair on the road, and the same night she arrived went up to the President. She demanded to know what Montgomery Blair had gone to Missouri for. Mr. Lincoln said he didn't know. 'Has he gone out to remove my husband?' said Mrs. Fremont. 'You cannot remove Gen. Fremont. He would not be removed.' Mr. Lincoln instantly began to talk about the difficulties of making a journey from St. Louis to Washington alone. Three or four times during the conversation she repeated, 'Gen. Fremont cannot be removed.' Lincoln evaded that part of the talk every time, and she left unsatisfied.

HOW HE BECAME PRESIDENT.

"Mr. Lincoln became President mainly on account of his debate with Douglas. He had never been in any great prominence as an office-holder. His thorough-going devotion to his party brought him universal good-will, however, and he grew so harmoniously into the advocacy of Republican principles and opposition to Douglas' notion of squatter sovereignty that there was a general desire to see him come forward and debate with Douglas. I can tell you something interesting about the debate. Lincoln had no money. He was in no position to match a man of Douglas' financial resources. The people in Lincoln's following, however, put their hands in their pockets and subscribed for a band of music to appear with him, and that band was procured in Indiana. They put the band on a wagon to send it by the roads from point to point of meeting. Douglas meantime came on to New York and borrowed $100,000.00. I think he got some of it from Ben Wood and Fernando Wood. He then took a special train of cars and made a sort of triumphal tour of the State, designing to carry the Senatorship by storm. Lincoln said after the contest was over, with a certain serious grimness, "I reckon that the campaign has cost me fully $250.' It was generally understood in the West that the same campaign cost Douglas $100,000. Lincoln's speeches against Douglas were extemporaneous, and he never revised them. My impression is that young McCullagh, now an editor in St. Louis, was the stenographer of Lincoln's speeches. Douglas did revise his remarks. They met seven times, if I remember. Lincoln reasoned so closely and carefully on Douglas' false statements that he came out of the campaign covered with respect, and instantly the movement started to make Lincoln President. I think it is due to Mr. Seward's memory to say that his extreme views on the slavery question helped to beat him.

VERY CARELESS.

"Lincoln was too careless. He would go out of his house at night and walk over to the War Department, where Stanton was receiving, dispatches, unattended. I said to him: 'Lincoln' you have no business to expose yourself in this way. It is known that you go out at midnight and return here sometimes at two o'clock in the morning from the War Department. It would be very easy to kill you.' The President replied that if anybody desired to assassinate him he did not suppose any amount of care would save him."

HIS PLAN OF RECONSTRUCTION.

"Lincoln would have made," says Mr. Usher, "a powerful white Republican party in every Southern State. He had that in him which would have made the Southern people support him in preference to the radical Northern politicians. Lincoln would have said in private to their leaders, 'You will have to stand in with me and help me out; otherwise Sumner and Stevens and those fellows will beat us both.' He would have said, 'You go back home and start some schools yourselves for the negroes, and put them on the route to citizenship. Let it be your own work. Make some arrangements to give them some land ultimately out of the public domain in your States. In that way you will have them your friends politically, and your prosperity will not be embarrassed.' Only Mr. Lincoln could have carried out this platform. His temperament, eminence and quality all adapted him for such a great part."

MR. LINCOLN'S IMPORTANT LETTER.

"Old time politicians," says a writer, "will readily recall the heated political campaign of 1843 in

11

the neighboring State of Illinois. The chief interest in the campaign lay in the race for Congress in the Capitol district, which was between Hardin—fiery, eloquent and impetuous Democrat; and Lincoln—plain, practical and ennobled Whig. The world knows the result. Lincoln was elected.

"It is not so much with his election as with the manner in which he secured his nomination with which we have to deal. Before that ever-memorable spring Lincoln vacillated between the courts of Springfield, rated as a plain, honest, logical Whig, with no ambition higher, politically, than to occupy some good home office. Late in the fall of 1842 his name began to be mentioned in connection with Congressional aspirations, which fact greatly annoyed the leaders of his political party, who had already selected as the Whig candidate, one Baker, afterward the gallant Colonel, who fell so bravely and died such an honorable death on the battlefield at Ball's Bluff, in 1862. Despite all efforts of his opponents within his party the name of the 'gaunt rail-splitter' was hailed with acclaim by the masses, to whom he had endeared himself by his witticisms, honest tongue, and quaint philosophy when on the stump or mingling with them in their homes.

"The convention, which met in early spring in the city of Springfield, was to be composed of the usual number of delegates. The contest for the nomination was spirited and exciting. A few weeks before the meeting of the convention the fact was found by the leaders that the advantage lay with Lincoln, and that, unless they pulled some very fine wires, nothing could save Baker. They attempted to play the game that has so often won, by 'convincing' delegates under instructions for Lincoln to violate them and vote for Baker. They had apparently succeeded. 'The plans of mice and men aft gang aglee;' so it was in this case. Two days before the convention Lincoln received an intimation of this, and late at night indited the following letter. The letter was addressed to Martin Morris, who resides at Petersburg, an intimate friend of his, and by him circulated among those who were instructed for him at the county convention. It had the desired effect. The convention meet, the scheme of the conpirators miscarried, Lincoln was nominated, made a vigorous canvass, and was triumphantly elected, thus paving the way for his more extended and brilliant conquests. This letter, Lincoln has often told his friends, gave him ultimately the Chief Magistracy of the Nation. He has also said that had he been beaten before the convention he would have been forever obscured. The following is a verbatim copy of the epistle:

"'April 14, 1843.—FRIEND MORRIS: I have heard it intimated that Baker has been attempting to get you or Miles, or both of you, to violate the instructions of the meeting that appointed you, and to go for him. I have insisted, and still insist, that this cannot be true. Surely Baker would not do the like. As well might Hardin ask me to vote for him in the convention. Again, it is said there will be an attempt to get up instructions in your county requiring you to go for Baker. This is all wrong. Upon the same rule, why might not I fly from the decision against me in Sangamon, and get up instruction to their delegates to go for me? There are at least 1,200 Whigs

13

in the county that took no part, and yet I would as soon stick my head in the fire as to attempt it. Besides, if anyone should get the nomination by such extraordinary means, all harmony in the district would inevitably be lost. Honest Whigs (and very nearly all of them are honest) would not quietly abide such enormities. I repeat, such an attempt on Baker's part cannot be true. Write me at Springfield how the matter is. Don't show or speak of this letter.'

"Mr. Morris did show the letter, and Mr. Lincoln always thanked his stars that he did."

MR. LINCOLN'S SECOND INAUGURAL ADDRESS.

(D elivered, March 4, 1865, at Washington.)

"Mr. Lincoln was re-inaugurated into the Presidential office on the fourth of March, 1865. An immense crowd was in attendance—a crowd of affectionate friends, not doubtful of the President, and not doubtful of one another and the future, as at the first inauguration. Chief Justice Chase administered the oath of office; and then Mr. Lincoln read his inaugural address concerning which it has been well said that it was a paper whose Christian sentiments and whose reverent and pious spirit has no parallel among the state papers of the American Presidents. I$_t$ showed the President still untouched by resentment^t still brotherly in his feelings toward the enemies o' the government, and still profoundy conscious of the overruling power of Providence in national affairs. The address was as follows:

"FELLOW-COUNTRYMEN:—At this second appearing to take the oath of the Presidential office, there is less occasion for an extended address than there was at the first. Then a statement somewhat in detail of a course to be pursued seemed very fitting and proper. Now, at the expiration of four years, during which public declarations have been constantly called forth on every point and phase of the great contest which still absorbs the attention and engrosses the energies of the nation, little that is new could be presented.

"The progress of our arms, upon which all else chiefly depends, is as well known to the public as to myself; and it is, I trust, reasonably satisfactory and encouraging to all. With high hope for the future, no prediction in regard to it is ventured.

"On the occasion corresponding to this four years ago, all thoughts were anxiously directed to an impending civil war. All dreaded it; all sought to avoid it. While the inaugural address was being delivered from this place, devoted altogether to saving the Union without war, insurgent agents were in the city seeking to destroy it without war—seeking to dissolve the Union and divide the effects by negotiation. Both parties deprecated war; but one of them would make war rather than let the nation survive, and the other would accept war rather than let it perish; and the war came. 'One eighth of the whole population were colored slaves, not distributed generally over the Union, but localized in the southern part of it. These slaves constituted a peculiar and powerful interest. All knew that this interest was somehow the cause of the war. To strengthen, perpetuate and extend this interest, was the object for

15

which the insurgents would rend the Union, even by war, while the government claimed no right to do more than to restrict the territorial enlargement of it.

"Neither party expected for the war the magnitude or the duration which it has already attained. Neither anticipated that the cause of the conflict might cease with, or even before, the conflict itself should cease. Each looked for an easier triumph, and a result less fundamental and astounding.

"Both read the same Bible and pray to the same God, and each invokes his aid against the other. It may seem strange that men should dare to ask a just God's assistance in wringing their bread from the sweat of other men's faces; but let us judge not, that we be not judged. The prayers of both could not be answered fully. The Almighty has his own purposes. 'Woe unto the world because of offense, for it must needs be that offenses come; but woe to that man by whom the offense cometh.' If we shall suppose that American slavery is one of these offenses, which in the providence of God must needs come, but which having continued through his appointed time, he now wills to remove, and that he gives to both North and South this terrible war as the woe due to those by whom the offense came, shall we discern therein any departure from those divine attributes which the believers in a living God always ascribe to him?

"Fondly do we hope, fervently do we pray, that this mighty scourge of war may soon pass away. Yet, if God wills that it continue until all the wealth piled by the bondsman's two hundred and fifty years of unrequited toil shall be sunk, and until every drop of blood drawn with the lash shall be paid with another drawn with the sword; as was said three thousand years ago, so still it must be said, 'The judgments of the Lord are true and righteous altogether.'

"With malice toward none, with charity for all, with firmness in the right, as God gives us to see the right, let us strive on to finish the work we are in, to bind up the nation's wounds, to care for him who shall have born, the battle and for his widow and or-phans, to do all which may achieve and cherish a just and a lasting peace among ourselves and with all nations."

THE UGLIEST MAN HE EVER MET.

It is said that Mr. Lincoln was always ready to join in a laugh at his own expense, concern-ing which he was indifferent. Many of his friends will recognize the following story —the incident hav-ing actually occurred—which Lincoln always told with great glee:

"In the days when I used to be 'on the circuit court,'" said Lincoln, "I was accosted in the cars by a stranger, who said:

"'Excuse me, sir, but I have an article in my possession which belongs to you.'

"'How is that?' I asked, considerably astonished.

"The stranger took a jack-knife from his pocket. 'This knife,' said he, 'was placed in my hands some years ago, with the injunction that I was to keep it until I found a man uglier than myself. I have car-ried it from that time to this. Allow me now to say, sir, that I think you are fairly entitled to the prop-erty.'"

MR. LINCOLN'S KINDNESS AND CONSIDERATION.

"President Lincoln," says the Hon. W. D. Kell, "was a large and many-sided man, and yet so simple that no one, not even a child, could approach him without feeling that he had found in him a sympathizing friend. I remember that I apprised Mr. Lincoln of the fact that a lad, the son of one of my townsmen, had served a year on board the gunboat *Ottawa*, and had been in two important engagements; in the first as a powder-monkey, when he conducted himself with such coolness that he had been chosen as captain's messenger in the second; and I suggested to the President that it was in his power to send to the Naval School, annually, three boys who had served at least a year in the navy.

"He at once wrote on the back of a letter from the commander of the *Ottawa*, which I had handed him, to the Secretary of the Navy: 'If the appointments for this year have not been made, let this boy be appointed.'

"The appointment had not been made, and I brought it home with me. It directed the lad to report for examination at the school in July. Just as he was ready to start, his father, looking over the law, discovered that he could not report until he was fourteen years of age, which he would not be until September following. The poor child sat down and wept. He feared that he was not to go to the Naval School. He was, however, soon consoled by being told that 'the President could make it right.' It was my fortune to meet him the next morning at the door of the Executive Chamber with his father.

"Taking by the hand the little fellow—short for his age, dressed in the sailor's blue pants and shirt—I advanced with him to the President, who sat in his usual seat, and said:

"'Mr. President, my young friend, Willie Bladen, finds a difficulty about his appointment. You have directed him to appear at the school in July; but he is not yet fourteen years of age.' But before I half finished, Mr. Lincoln, laying down his spectacles, rose and said:

"'Bless me! is that the boy who did so gallantly in those two great battles? Why, I feel that I should bow to him, and not he to me.' The little fellow had made his graceful bow.

"The President took the papers at once, and as soon as he learned that a postponement until September would suffice, made the order that the lad should report in that month. Then putting his hand on Willie's head, he said:

"'Now, my boy, go home and have good fun during the two months, for they are about the last holiday you will get.' The little fellow bowed himself out, feeling that the President of the United States, though a very great man, was one that he would nevertheless like to have a game of romps with."

GAVE A RIGHTFUL DECISION.

Attorney-General Bates was once remonstrating with the President against the appointment of a western man of indifferent reputation as a lawyer to a judicial position of considerable importance.

"Well, now, Judge," returned Mr. Lincoln, "I think you are rather too hard on ——. Besides that, I must

19

tell you, he did me a good turn long ago. When I took to the law, I was walking to court one morning, with some ten or twelve miles of bad road before me, when —— overtook me in his wagon.

"'Hallo, Lincoln!' said he; 'going to the court-house? Come in and I will give you a seat.'

"Well, I got in, and —— went on reading his papers. Presently the wagon struck a stump on one side of the road; then it hopped off to the other. I looked out and saw the driver was jerking from side to side in his seat; so said I, 'Judge, I think your coachman has been taking a drop too much this morning.'

"'Well, I declare, Lincoln,' said he, 'I should not much wonder if you are right, for he has nearly upset me half a dozen times since starting. So, putting his head out of the window, he shouted, '*Why, you infernal scoundrel, you are drunk!*'

"Upon which, pulling up his horses and turning round with great gravity, the coachman said, 'Be dad! but that's the first *rightful decision your honor has given for the last twelve months!*'"

GOD WANTED THE CHURCH FOR SOLDIERS.

"Among the numerous applicants who visited the White House one day was a well-dressed lady. She came forward, without apparent embarrassment in her air or manner, and addressed the President. Giving her a very close and scrutinizing look, he said:

"'Well, madam, what can I do for you?'

"She told him that she lived in Alexandria; that

20

the church where she worshiped had been taken for a hospital.

"'What church, madam?' Mr. Lincoln asked, in a quick, nervous manner.

"'The —— Church,' she replied; 'and as there are only two or three wounded soldiers in it, I came to see if you would not let us have it, as we want it very much to worship God in.'

"'Madam, have you been to see the Post Surgeon at Alexandria about this matter?'

"'Yes, sir; but we could do nothing with him.'

"'Well, we put him there to attend to just such business, and it is reasonable to suppose that he knows better what should be done under the circumstances than I do. See here: you say you live in Alexandria; probably you own property there. How much will you give to assist in building a hospital?'

"'You know, Mr. Lincoln, our property is very much embarrassed by the war;—so, really, I could hardly afford to give much for such a purpose.'

"'Well, madam, I expect we shall have another fight soon; and my candid opinion is, God *wants that church for poor wounded Union soldiers* as much as He does for secesh people to worship in.' Turning to his table, he said, quite abruptly, 'You will excuse me; I can do nothing for you. Good-day, madam.'"

SIGNING EMANCIPATION PROCLAMATION.

"The Emancipation Proclamation was taken to Mr. Lincoln at noon on the first day of January, 1865, by Secretary Seward and Frederick his son. As it lay unrolled before him, Mr. Lincoln took a pen, dipped it in ink, moved his hand to the place for the signature, held it a moment, and then removed his hand and dropped the pen. After a little hesitation he again took up the pen and went through the same movement as before. Mr. Lincoln then turned to Mr. Seward, and said:

"'I have been shaking hands since nine o'clock this morning, and my right arm is almost paralyzed. If my name ever goes into history it will be for this act, and my whole soul is in it. If my hand trembles when I sign the Proclamation, all who examine the document hereafter will say, "He hesitated."'"

"He then turned to the table, took up the pen again, slowly, and firmly wrote 'Abraham Lincoln,' with which the whole world is now familiar. He then looked up, smiled, and said: *That will do.*'

MR. LINCOLN AND THE DAREY BOY.

"Once, in Springfield, I was going off on a short journey, and reached the depot a little ahead of time. Leaning against the fence, just outside the depot, was a little darkey boy whom I knew, named 'Dick,' busily digging with his toe in a mud-puddle. As I came up, I said, 'Dick, what are you about?'

'Making a *church*,' said he.

"'A church?' said I; 'what do you mean?'

"'Why, yes,' said Dick, pointing with his toe, 'don't you see? there is the shape of it; there's the steps and front door —here the pews, where the folks set— and there's the pulpit.'

"'Yes, I see,' said I, 'but why don't you make a minister?'

"'Laws,' answered Dick, with a grin, 'I hain't got *mud* enough!'"

A SOMEWHAT DOUBTFUL ABUTMENT.

In Abbott's "History of the Civil War," the following story is told as one of Lincoln's "hardest hits:" "I once knew," said Lincoln, "a sound churchman by the name of Brown, who was a member of a very sober and pious committee having in charge the erection of a bridge over a dangerous and rapid river. Several architects failed, and at last Brown said he had a friend named Jones, who had built several bridge and undoubtedly could build that one. So Mr. Jones was called in.

"'Can you build this bridge?' inquired the committee.

"'Yes,' replied Jones, 'or any other. I could build a bridge to the infernal regions, if necessary!'

"The committee were shocked, and Brown felt called upon to defend his friend. 'I know Jones so well,' said he, 'and he is so honest a man and so good an architect, that if he states soberly and positively that he can build a bridge to—to—why, I believe it; but I feel bound to say that I have my doubts about the abutment on the infernal side.'

"So," said Mr. Lincoln, "when politicians told me that the northern and southern wings of the Democracy could be harmonized, why, I believed them, of course; but I always had my doubts about the 'abutment' on the *other side*."

MR. LINCOLN'S POWERS OF ENDURANCE.

"On the Monday before the assassination, when the President was on his return from Richmond, he stopped at City Point. Calling upon the head surgeon

23

at that place, Mr. Lincoln told him that he wished to visit all the hospitals under his charge, and shake hands with every soldier. The surgeon asked if he knew what he was undertaking, there being five or six thousand soldiers at that place, and it would be quite a tax upon his strength to visit all the wards and shake hands with every soldier. Mr. Lincoln answered, with a smile, he 'guessed he was equal to the task; at any rate he would try, and go as far as he could; he should never, probably, see the boys again, and he wanted them to know that he appreciated what they had done for their country.'

"Finding it useless to try to dissuade him, the surgeon began his rounds with the President, who walked from bed to bed, extending his hand to all, saying a few words of sympathy to some, making kind inquiries of others, and welcomed by all with the heartiest cordiality.

"As they passed along, they came to a ward in which lay a rebel who had been wounded and was then a prisoner. As the tall figure of the kindly visitor appeared in sight, he was recognized by the rebel soldier who, raising himself on his elbow in bed, watched Mr. Lincoln as he approached and, extending his hand, exclaimed while tears ran down his cheeks:

"'Mr. Lincoln, I have long wanted to see you, to ask your forgiveness for ever raising my hand against the old flag.'

"Mr. Lincoln was moved to tears. He heartily shook the hand of the repentant rebel, and assured him of his good-will, and with a few words of kind advice passed on. After some hours the tour of the various hospitals was made, and Mr. Lincoln returned with the soldier to his office. They had scarcely entered, however, when a messenger boy came saying that one ward had been omitted, and 'the boys wanted to see the President. The surgeon, who was thoroughly tired, and knew Mr. Lincoln must be, tried to dissuade him from going; but the good man said he must go back; he would not knowingly omit one; 'the boys' would be so disappointed. So he went with the messenger, accompanied by the surgeon, and shook hands with the gratified soldiers, and then returned again to the office.

"The surgeon expressed the fear that the President's arm would be lamed with so much hand-shaking, saying that it certainly must ache. Mr. Lincoln smiled, and saying something about his 'strong muscles,' stepped out at the open door, took up a very large, heavy axe which lay there by a log of wood, and chopped vigorously for a few moments, sending the chips flying in all directions; and then, pausing, he extended his right arm to its full length, holding the axe out horizontally, without its even quivering as he held it. Strong men who looked on—men accustomed to manual labor—could not hold the same axe in that position for a moment. Returning to the office, he took a glass of lemonade, for he would take no stronger beverage; and while he was within, the chips he had chopped were gathered up and safely cared for by a hospital steward, because they were 'the chips that Father Abraham chopped.'"

LINCOLN ADOPTS STANTON'S SUGGESTION.

"One night the Secretary of War, with others of the Cabinet, were in the company of the President, at the Capitol, awaiting the passage of the final bills of Congress. In the intervals of reading and signing these documents, the military situation was considered—the lively conversation tinged by the confident and glowing account of General Grant, of his mastery of the position, and of his belief that a few days more would see Richmond in their possession, and the army of Lee either dispersed utterly or captured bodily—when the telegram from Grant was received, saying that Lee had asked an interview with reference to peace. Mr. Lincoln was elated, and the kindness of his heart was manifest in intimations of favorable terms to be granted to the conquered rebels.

"Stanton listened in silence, restraining his emotion, but at length the tide burst forth. 'Mr. President,' said he, 'to-morrow is inauguration day. If you are not to be the President of an obedient and united people, you had better not be inaugurated. Your work is already done, if any other authority than yours is for one moment to be recognized, or any terms made that do not signify you are the supreme head of the nation. If generals in the field are to negotiate peace, or any other chief magistrate is to be acknowledged on this continent, then you are not needed, and you had better not take the oath of office.'

"'Stanton, you are right!' said the President, his whole tone changing. 'Let me have a pen.'

"Mr. Lincoln sat down at the table, and wrote as follows:

"'The President directs me to say to you that he wished you to have no conference with General Lee, unless it be for the capitulation of Lee's army, or on some minor or military matter. He instructs me to say that you are not to decide, discuss, or confer upon any political question. Such questions the President holds in his own hands, and will submit them to no military conferences or conventions. In the meantime you are to press to the utmost your military advantages.'

"The President read over what he had written, and then said:

"'Now, Stanton, date and sign this paper, and send it to Grant. We'll see about this peace business.'

"The duty was discharged only too gladly by the energetic Secretary."

HE DID NOT GET THE PASS.

"Judge Baldwin, of California, being in Washington, called one day on General Halleck, and, presuming upon a familiar acquaintance in California a few years before, solicited a pass outside of our lines to see a brother in Virginia, not thinking that he would meet with a refusal, as both his brother and himself were good Union men.

"'We have been deceived too often,' said General Halleck, 'and I regret I can't grant it.'

"Judge B. then went to Stanton, and was very briefly disposed of, with the same result. Finally, he obtained an interview with Mr. Lincoln, and stated his case.

"'Have you applied to General Halleck?' inquired the President.

"'Yes, and met with a flat refusal,' said Judge B.

"'Then you must see Stanton,' continued the President.

"'I have, and with the same result,' was the reply.

"'Well, then,' said Mr. Lincoln, with a smile, 'I can do nothing; for you must know *that I have very little influence with this Administration.*'"

THE SWEARING WAS NECESSARY THEN.

"General Fisk, attending the reception at the White House, on one occasion saw, waiting in the ante-room, a poor old man from Tennessee. Sitting down beside him, he inquired his errand, and learned that he had been waiting three or four days to get an audience, and that on seeing Mr. Lincoln probably depended the life of his son, who was under sentence of death for some military offense.

"General Fisk wrote his case in outline on a card, and sent it in, with a special request that the President would see the man. In a moment the order came; and past senators, governors and generals, waiting impatiently, the old man went into the President's presence.

"He showed Mr. Lincoln his papers, and he, on taking them, said he would look into the case and give him the result on the following day.

"'To-morrow may be too late! My son is under sentence of death! The decision ought to be made now!' and the streaming tears told how much he was moved.

"'Come,' said Mr. Lincoln, 'wait a bit, and I'll tell you a story;' and then he told the old man General Fisk's story about the swearing driver, as follows:

The General had begun his military life as a Colonel, and, when he raised his regiment in Missouri, he proposed to his men that he should do all the swearing of the regiment. They assented; and for months no instance was known of the violation of the promise. The Colonel had a teamster named John Todd, who, as roads were not always the best, had some difficulty in commanding his temper and his tongue. John happened to be driving a mule-team through a series of mud-holes a little worse than usual, when, unable to restrain himself any longer, he burst forth into a volley of energetic oaths. The Colonel took notice of the offense, and brought John to an account.

"John," said he, "didn't you promise to let me do all the swearing of the regiment?"

"Yes, I did, Colonel," he replied, but "the fact was the swearing had to be done *then* or not at all, and *you were not there to do it.*"

As he told the story, the old man forgot his boy, and both the President and his listener had a hearty laugh together at its conclusion. Then he wrote a few words which the old man read, and in which he found new occasion for tears; but these tears were tears of joy, for the words saved the life of his son."

ADVICE TO A BACHELOR AMBASSADOR.

"Upon the betrothal of the Prince of Wales to the Princess Alexandria, Queen Victoria sent a letter to each of the European sovereigns, and also to President Lincoln, announcing the fact. Lord Lyons, her ambassador at Washington,—a "bachelor," by the way,—requested an audience of Mr. Lincoln, that he might present this important document in person. At the time appointed he was received at the White House, in company with Mr. Seward.

"'May it please your Excellency,' said Lord Lyons,

"I hold in my hand an autograph letter from my royal mistress, Queen Victoria, which I have been commanded to present to your Excellency. In it she informs your Excellency, that her son, his Royal Highness the Prince of Wales, is about to contract a matrimonial alliance with her Royal Highness the Princess Alexandria of Denmark.'

After continuing in this strain for a few minutes, Lord Lyons tendered the letter to the President and awaited his reply. It was short, simple, and expressive, and consisted simply of the words:

"'Lord Lyons, *go thou and do likewise.*'

"It is doubtful if an English ambassador was ever addressed in this manner before, and it would be interesting to learn what success he met with in putting the reply in diplomatic language when he reported it to her Majesty."

MR. LINCOLN AS A HORSE TRADER.

"When Abraham Lincoln was a lawyer in Illinois, he and a certain Judge once got to bantering one another about trading horses; and it was agreed that the next morning at 9 o'clock they should make a trade, the horse to be unseen up to that hour, and no backing out, under a forfeiture of $25.00.

At the hour appointed the Judge came up, leading the sorriest looking specimen of a horse ever seen in those parts. In a few minutes Mr. Lincoln was seen approaching with a wooden saw-horse upon his shoulders. Great were the shouts and the laughter of the crowd, and both were greatly increased when Mr. Lincoln, on surveying the Judge's animal, set down his saw-horse, and exclaimed: 'Well, Judge, this is the first time I ever got the worst of it in a horse trade.'"

HIS FIRST SPEECH.

"The following first speech of Abraham Lincoln was delivered at Poppsville, Ill., just after the close of a public sale, at which time and in those early days speaking was in order. Mr. Lincoln was then but twenty-three years of age, but being called for, mounted a stump and gave a concise statement of his policy:

"'Gentlemen, Fellow-citizens: I presume you know who I am. I am humble Abraham Lincoln. I have been solicited by many friends to become a candidate for the legislature. My politics can be briefly stated. I am in favor of the internal improvement system, and a high protective tariff. These are my sentiments and political principles. If elected, I shall be thankful. If not, it will be all the same.'"

HIS FIRST FIVE HUNDRED DOLLARS.

"Soon after Mr. Lincoln entered upon his profession at Springfield, he was engaged in a criminal case, in which it was thought there was little chance of success. Throwing all his powers into it, he came off victorious, and promptly received for his services five hundred dollars. A legal friend, calling upon him the next morning, found him sitting before a table, upon which his money was spread out, counting it over and over.

"'Look here, Judge,' said Lincoln; 'see what a heap of money I've got from the —— case. Did you ever see anything like it? Why, I never had so much money in my life before, put it all together' Then crossing his arms upon the table, his manner sobering down, he added, 'I have got just five hundred dollars: if it were only seven hundred and fifty, I would go directly and purchase a quarter section of land, and settle it upon my old step-mother.'

"His friend said that if the deficiency was all he needed he would loan him the amount, taking his note, to which Mr. Lincoln instantly acceded.

"His friend then said: 'Lincoln, I would not do just what you have indicated. Your step-mother is getting old, and will not probably live many years. I would settle the property upon her for her use during her lifetime, to revert to you upon her death.'

"With much feeling, Mr. Lincoln replied: 'I shall do no such thing. It is a poor return, at the best, for all the good woman's devotion and fidelity to me, and there is not going to be any half-way business about it; and so saying, he gathered up his money and proceeded forthwith to carry his long-cherished purpose into execution."

HOW HONEST ABE DIVIDED MONEY.

"A little fact in Lincoln's work will illustrate his ever present desire to deal honestly and justly with men. He had always a partner in his professional life, and, when he went out upon the circuit, this partner was usually at home. While out, he frequently took up and disposed of cases that were never entered at the office. In these cases, after receiving his fees, he divided the money in his pocket-book, labeling each sum (wrapped in a piece of paper), that belonged to his partner, stating his name, and the case on which it was received. He could not be content to keep an account. He divided the money, so that if he, by an casualty, should fail of an opportunity to pay it over, there could be no dispute as to the exact amount that was his partner's due. This may seem trivial, nay, boyish, but it was like Mr. Lincoln."

MR. LINCOLN'S CHARITABLE NATURE.

"It was not possible for Mr. Lincoln to regard his clients simply in the light of business. An unfortunate man was the subject of his sympathy. A Mr. Cogdal, who related this instance to Mr. Holland, met with a financial wreck in 1843. He employed Mr. Lincoln as his lawyer, and at the close of the business, gave him a note to cover the regular lawyer's fees. He was soon after blown up by an accidental discharge of powder, and lost his hand. Meeting Mr. Lincoln sometime after the accident, on the steps of the State House, the kind lawyer asked him how he was getting along.

"'Badly enough,' replied Mr. Cogdal, 'I am both broken up in business and crippled.' Then he added, 'I have been thinking about that note of yours.'

"Mr. Lincoln, who had probably known all about Mr. Cogdal's troubles and had prepared himself for the meeting, took out his pocket-book, and saying, with a laugh, 'Well, you needn't think anything more about it,' handed him the note.

"Mr. Cogdal protesting, Mr. Lincoln said, 'If you had the money, I wouldn't take it,' and hurried away.

"At this same date, he was frankly writing about his poverty to his friends, as a reason for not making them a visit, and probably found it no easy task to

33

take care of his family, even when board at the Globe
Tavern was 'only four dollars a week.'"

MR. LINCOLN'S LEGAL ACUMEN.

"Senator McDonald states that he saw a jury trial
in Illinois, at which Lincoln defended an old man
charged with assault and battery. No blood had
been spilled, but there was malice in the prosecution
and the chief witness was eager to make the most of
it. On cross-examination, Lincoln gave him rope
and drew him out; asked him how long the fight
lasted, and how much ground it covered. The witness thought the fight must have lasted an hour, and
covered an acre of ground. Lincoln called his attention to the fact that nobody was hurt, and then, with
an inimitable air, asked him if he didn't think it was
a mighty small crop for an acre of ground.' The
jury rejected the case with contempt as beneath the
dignity of twelve brave, good men and true.

"In another case the son of his old friend, who had
employed him and loaned him books, was charged
with a murder committed in a riot at a camp meeting. Lincoln volunteered for the defense. A witness swore that he saw the prisoner strike the fatal
blow. It was night, but he swore that the full moon
was shining clear, and he saw everything distinctly.
The case seemed hopeless, but Lincoln produced an
almanac, and showed that at the hour named there was
no moon. Then he depicted the crime of perjury with
such eloquence that the false witness fled the Court
House. One who heard the trial says that it was near
night when he concluded, saying: 'If justice was
done, before the sun set it would shine upon his client
a free man.'

"The Court charged the jury; they retired, and presently returned a verdict—'Not guilty.' The prisoner fell weeping into his mother's arms, and then turned to thank Mr. Lincoln, who, looking out at the sun, said: 'It is not yet sundown, and you are free.'"

THE SHIELDS-LINCOLN DUEL.

"The late Gen. Shields was Auditor of the State of Illinois in 1839. While he occupied this important office he was involved in an 'affair of honor' with a Springfield lawyer—no less a personage than Abraham Lincoln. At this time, 'James Shields, Auditor,' was the pride of the young Democracy, and was considered a dashing fellow by all, the ladies included. In the summer of 1842 the Springfield *Journal* contained some letters from the 'Lost Township,' by a contributor whose nom de plume was 'Aunt Becca,' which held up the gallant young Auditor as 'a ball-room dandy, floatin' about on the earth without heft or substance, just like a lot of cat-fur where cats had been fightin'.'

"These letters caused intense excitement in the town. Nobody knew or guessed their authorship. Shields swore it would be coffee and pistols for two if he should find out who had been lampooning him so unmercifully. Thereupon 'Aunt Becca' wrote another letter, which made the furnace of his wrath seven times hotter than before, in which she made a very humble apology, and offered to let him squeeze her hand for satisfaction, adding:

"'If this should not answer, there is one thing more I would rather do than to get a lickin'. I have all along expected to die a widow; but as Mr. Shields

35

is rather good looking than otherwise, I must say I
don't car£ if we compromise the matter by—really,
Mr. Printer, I can't help blushin'—but I—must come
out—I—but widowed modesty—well, if I must, I
must,—wouldn't he—maybe sorter let the old grudge
drap if I was to consent to be—be—his wife. I know
he is a fightin' man, and would rather fight than eat;
but isn't marryin' better than fightin', though it does
sometimes run into it? And I don't think, upon the
whole, I'd be sich a bad match, neither; I'm not
over sixty, and am jest four feet three in my bare feet,
and not much more round the girth; and for color,
I wouldn't turn my back to nary girl in the Lost
Townships. But, after all, maybe I'm countin' my
chickens before they're hatched, and dreamin' of
matrimonial bliss when the only alternative reserved
for me may be a lickin'. Jeff tells me the way these
fire-eaters do is to give the challenged party the
choice of weapons, which being the case, I tell you
in confidence, I never fight with anything but broom-
sticks or hot water, or a shovelful of coals or some
such thing; the former of which being somewhat
like a shillalah, may not be so very objectionable to
him. I will give him a choice, however, in one thing,
and that is whether, when we fight, I shall wear
breeches or he petticoats, for I presume this change
is sufficient to place us on an equality.'

"Of course someone had to shoulder the responsibility of these letters after such a shot. The real
author was none other than Miss Mary Todd, afterward the wife of Abraham Lincoln, to whom she was
engaged, and who was in honor bound to assume, for
belligerent purposes, the responsibility of her sharp
pen-thrusts. Mr. Lincoln accepted the situation

Not long after the two men, with their seconds, were on their way to the field of honor. But the affair was fixed up without any fighting, and thus ended in a fizzle the Lincoln-Shields duel of the Lost Townships."

MR. LINCOLN TELLS A SECRET.

"When the Sherman expedition which captured Port Royal went out, there was a general curiosity to know where it had gone   A person visiting President Lincoln at his official residence importuned him to disclose the destination.

"'Will you keep it entirely secret?' asked the President.   .

"'Oh yes, upon my honor.'

"'Well, said the President, I'll tell you.'   Assuming an air of great mystery, and drawing the man close to him, he kept him a moment awaiting the revelation with an open mouth and in great anxiety, and then said in a loud whisper, which was heard all over the room, 'The expedition has gone to—sea.'"

HIS NOISE DIDN'T HURT ANYBODY.

"When General Phelps took possession of Ship Island, near New Orleans, early in the war, it will be remembered that he issued a proclamation, somewhat bombastic in tone, freeing the slaves.   To the surprise of many people, on both sides, the President took no official notice of this movement.   Some time had elapsed, when one day a friend took him to task for his seeming indifference on so important a matter.

'Well,' said Mr. Lincoln, 'I feel about that a good deal as a man whom I will call 'Jones,' whom I once knew, did about his wife. He was one of your meek men, and had the reputation of being badly henpecked. At last, one day his wife was seen switching him out of the house. A day or two afterward a friend met him on the street, and said: 'Jones, I have always stood up for you, as you know; but I am not going to do it any longer. Any man who will stand quietly and take a switching from his wife, deserves to be horsewhipped.' Jones looked up with a wink, patting his friend on the back. 'Now *don't*,' said he; 'why, it didn't *hurt* me any; and you've no idea what a *power* of *good* it did Sarah Ann'"

HE PREFERRED GRANT'S WHISKY.

"Just previous to the fall of Vicksburg, a self-constituted committee, solicitous for the *morale* of our armies, took it upon themselves to visit the President and urge the removal of General Grant.

In some surprise Mr. Lincoln inquired, 'For what reason?'

"'Why,' replied the spokesman, 'he drinks too much whisky.'

"'Ah!' rejoined Mr. Lincoln, dropping his lower lip. "By the way, gentlemen, can either of you tell me where General Grant procures his whisky? because, if I can find out, I will send every general in the field *a barrel of it!*'"

AN APPROPRIATE ILLUSTRATION.

"At the White House one day some gentlemen were present from the West, excited and troubled about the commissions or omissions of the Administration. The President heard them patiently, and then replied: 'Gentlemen, suppose all the property you were worth was in gold, and you had put it in the hands of Blondin to carry across the Niagara River on a rope, would you shake the cable, or keep shouting out to him, 'Blondin, stand up a little straighter—Blondin, stoop a little more—go a little faster—lean a little more to the north—lean a little more to the south!' No! you would hold your breath as well as your tongue, and keep your hands off until he was safely over. The Government are carrying an immense weight. Untold treasures are in their hands. They are doing the very best they can. Don't badger them. Keep silence, and they'll get you safely across.'"

HE SWORE LIKE MR. SEWARD.

"Secretary Seward was an Episcopalian. On one of the occasions when President Lincoln's patience was tried by a self-appointed adviser who got warm and used strong language, Mr. Lincoln interrupted him by saying: 'You are an Episcopalian, aren't you?' And when asked why he thought so, said: 'You swear just like Mr. Seward, and he is.' This was Mr. Lincoln's way of getting rid of such advisers."

THE GLOVES KNOCKED THEM OUT.

"Mr. Lincoln's habits at the White House were as simple as they were at his old home in Illinois. He never alluded to himself as 'President,' or as occupying 'the Presidency.' His office, he always designated as 'this place.' 'Call me Lincoln,' said he to a friend—'Mr. President' had become so very tiresome to him. 'If you see a newsboy down the street, send him up this way,' said he to a passenger, as he stood waiting for the morning news at his gate. Friends cautioned him against exposing himself so openly in the midst of enemies; but he never heeded them. He frequently walked the streets at night, entirely unprotected; and he felt any check upon his free movements as a great annoyance. He delighted to see his familiar Western friends; and he gave them always a cordial welcome. He met them on the old footing, and fell at once into the accustomed habits of talk and story-telling.

"An old acquaintance, with his wife, visited Washington. Mr. and Mrs. Lincoln proposed to these friends to ride in the Presidential carriage. It should be stated, in advance, that the two men had probably never seen each other with gloves on in their lives, unless they were used as protection from the cold.

"The question of each—Mr. Lincoln at the White House, and his friend at the hotel—was, whether he should wear gloves. Of course, the ladies urged gloves; but Mr. Lincoln only put his in his pocket, to be used or not, according to circumstances.

"When the Presidential party arrived at the hotel, to take in their friends, they found the gentleman, overcome by his wife's persuasions, very handsomely gloved. The moment he took his seat, he began to draw off the clinging kids, while Mr. Lincoln began to draw his on!

"'No! no! no!' protested his friend, tugging at his

gloves. 'It is none of my doings; put up your gloves, Mr. Lincoln."

"So the two old friends were on even and easy terms, and had their ride after their old fashion."

TRIPLETS NAMED BY MR. LINCOLN.

"In South Starksboro, Addison County, Vt., according to the Burlington *Free Press*, there are residing triplets, sons of Leonard Haskins, born May 24, 1864, and named by President Lincoln. They have in their possession a letter from the hand of the martyr-President, and the names given were Abraham Lincoln, Gideon Welles and Simon Cameron. They are the children of American parents (who are still living) of limited circumstances, and have led a very retired life; are robust, intelligent, and moral, and have always been abstainers from liquor and profanity. There is an almost perfect resemblance between two, who are light complexioned, while the other is a striking contrast, having dark hair and eyes."

A PERVERTED PASSWORD

"An amusing story is attributed to President Lincoln, about the Iowa First, and the changes which a certain password underwent about the time of the battle of Springfield.

"One of the Dubuque officers, whose duty it was to furnish the guards with a password for the night, gave the word 'Potomac.' A German on guard, not comprehending distinctly the difference between B's and P's, understood it to be 'Bottomic,' and this, on being transferred to another, was corrupted into 'Buttermilk.' Soon afterward the officer who had given the word wished to return through the lines, and on approaching a sentinel was ordered to halt and the word demanded. He gave the word 'Potomac.'

"'Nicht right; you don't pass mit me dis way.'

"'But this is the word, and I will pass.'

"'No, you stan',"" at the same time placing a bayonet at his breast, in a manner that told the officer that 'Potomac' didn't pass in Missouri.

"'What is the word, then?'

"'Buttermilk.'

"'Well, then, buttermilk.'

"'Dat is right; you pass mit yourself all about your piziness.'

"There was then a general overhauling of the password and, the difference between Potomac and Buttermilk being understood, the joke became one of the laughable incidents of the campaign."

NO SPECIAL TRAIN FOR HINX.

"One of the last stories heard from Mr. Lincoln was concerning John Tyler, for whom it was to be expected, as an old Henry Clay Whig, he would entertain no great respect. 'A year or two after Tyler's accession to the Presidency,' said he, 'contemplating an excursion in some direction, his son went to order a special train of cars. It so happened that the railroad superintendent was a very strong Whig. On Bob's making known his errand, that official bluntly informed him that his road did not run any special trains for the President.

"'What!' said Bob, 'did you not furnish a special train for the funeral of General Harrison?'

"'Yes,' said the superintendent, stroking his whiskers; 'and if you will only bring your father here in *that* shape, you shall have the best train on the road!'"

HIS TITLES AT A DISCOUNT.

"Concerning a drollery of President Lincoln, this story is told:

"During the Rebellion an Austrian Count applied to President Lincoln for a position in the army. Being introduced by the Austrian Minister, he needed, of course, no further recommendation; but, as if fearing that his importance might not be duly appreciated, he proceeded to explain that he was a Count; that his family were ancient and highly respectable; when Lincoln, with a merry twinkle in his eye, tapping the aristocratic lover of titles on the shoulder, in a fatherly way, as if the man had confessed to some wrong, interrupted in a soothing tone, 'Never mind; you shall be treated with just as much consideration for all that'"

MORE LIGHT AND LESS NOISE

"An editorial, in a New York journal, opposing Lincoln's renomination, is said to have called out from him the following story: A traveler on the frontier found himself out of his reckoning one night in a most inhospitable region. A terrific thunder-storm came up, to add to his trouble. He floundered along until at length his horse gave out. The lightning afforded him the only clue to his way, but the peals of thunder were frightful. One bolt, which seemed to crash the earth beneath him, brought him to his

knees. By no means a praying man, his petition
was short and to the point—'O Lord, if it is all the
same to you, give us a little *more light and a little
less noise!'*"

STANTON ADVISED TO PREPARE FOR
DEATH.

"The imperious Stanton, when Secretary of War,
took a fancy one day to a house in Washington that
Lamon had just bargained for. He ordered the latter to vacate instanter. Lamon not only did not
vacate, but went to Stanton and said he would kill
him if he interfered with the house. Stanton was
furious at the threat, and made it known at once to
Lincoln. The latter said to the astonished War Secretary:

"'Well, Stanton, if Ward has said he will kill you,
he certainly will, and I'd advise you to prepare for
death without further delay.'

"The President promised, however, to do what he
could to appease the murderous Marshal, and this
was the end of Stanton's attempt on the house."

MR. LINCOLN'S APT REPLY.

"Lincoln's opponent for the Legislature in 1836 was
the Hon. Geo. Forquer, of Springfield, Ill., who was
celebrated for having introduced the first and only
lightning-rod in Springfield at this time. He said in
a speech, in Lincoln's presence, 'this young man
(Lincoln) would have to be taken down, and I am
sorry the task devolves upon me;' and then proceeded
to try and 'take him down.' Mr. Lincoln made a

reply, and in closing, turned to the crowd and made these remarks:

"'Fellow-Citizens:—It is for you, not for me, to say whether I am up, or down. The gentleman has alluded to my being a young man; I am older in years than I am in the tricks and trades of politicians. I desire to live, and desire place and distinction as a politician; but I would rather die now than, like the gentleman, live to see the day that I would have to erect a lightning-rod to protect a guilty conscience from an offended God.'"

MR. LINCOLN'S DEDICATION SPEECH AT GETTYSBURG.

(Delivered at the dedication of the Gettysburg National Cemetery, on the Gettysburg battle-field, Nov. 19, 1863.)

"Ladies and Gentlemen:—Fourscore and seven years ago our fathers brought forth upon this continent a new nation, conceived in liberty, and dedicated to the proposition that all men are created equal. Now we are engaged in a great civil war, testing whether that nation, or any nation so conceived and so dedicated, can long endure. We are met on a great battle-field of that war. We have come to dedicate a portion of that field as a final resting-place for those who here gave their lives that that nation might live. It is altogether fitting and proper that we should do this.

"But in a larger sense we cannot dedicate, we cannot consecrate, we cannot hallow this ground. The brave men, living and dead, who struggled here, have consecrated it far above our power to add or detract. The world will little note, nor long remember, what we say here; but it can never forget what they did here.

"It is for us, the living, rather to be dedicated here to the unfinished work which they who fought here have thus far so nobly advanced. It is rather for us to be here dedicated to the great task remaining before, that from those honored dead we take increased devotion to the cause for which they gave the last full measure of devotion; that we here highly resolve that these dead shall not have died in vain; that this nation, under God, shall have a new birth of freedom, and *that the government of the people, by the people, and for the people, shall not perish from the earth.*"

DRANK NOTHING BUT ADAM'S ALE.

"Immediately after Mr. Lincoln's nomination for President at the Chicago Convention, a committee, of which Governor Morgan, of New York, was Chairman, visited him in Springfield, Ill., where he was officially informed of his nomination.

"After this ceremony had passed, Mr. Lincoln remarked to the company, that as an appropriate conclusion to an interview so important and interesting as that which had just transpired, he supposed good manners would require that he should treat the committee with something to drink; and opening a door that led into a room in the rear, he called out, 'Mary! Mary!' A girl responded to the call, to whom Mr. Lincoln spoke a few words in an undertone, and, closing the door, returned to converse with his guests. In a few minutes the maiden entered, bearing a large waiter, containing several glass tumblers, and a large pitcher in the midst, and placed it upon the center-table. Mr. Lincoln arose, and gravely addressing the company, said: 'Gentlemen, we must pledge our mutual healths in the most healthy beverage which God has given to man—it is the only beverage I have ever used or allowed in my family, and I cannot con-scientiously depart from it on the present occasion—it is pure Adam's ale from the spring;' and, taking a tumbler, he touched it to his lips, and pledged them his highest respects in a cup of *cold water*. Of course, all his guests were constrained to admire his consis-tency, and to join in his example."

WOULD NOT COME A SECOND TIME.

"Among the visitors on one of the President's re-ception days, was a party of Congressmen, among whom was the Hon. Thomas Shannon, of California. Soon after the customary greeting, Mr. Shannon said:

"'Mr. President, I met an old friend of yours in California last summer, Thomas Campbell, who had a good deal to say of your Springfield life.'

"'Ah!' returned Mr. Lincoln, 'I am glad to hear of him. Campbell used to be a dry fellow,' he contin-ued. 'For a time he was Secretary of State. One day, during the legislative vacation, a meek, cadav-erous-looking man, with a white neck-cloth, intro-duced himself to him at his office, and, stating that he had been informed that Mr. C. had the letting of the Assembly Chamber, said that he wished to secure it, if possible, for a course of lectures he desired to deliver in Springfield.

"'May I ask,'said the Secretary, 'what is to be the subject of your lectures?'

A POEM BY LINCOLN.

In the April, 1894, number of the *Century* John (
Nicolay writes of "Lincoln's Literary Experiments
and quotes a poem written by the President in h
young manhood.   In a letter enclosing the poem
a friend, Lincoln explains that the ver es were writte
in 1844, when he visited the neighborhood in whic
he was raised, on a stumping tour.   Here are tl
opening stanzas:

> My childhood's home I see again,
>   And sadden with the view;
> And still, as memory crowds my brain,
>   There's pleasure in it, too.
>
> O Memory! thou midway world
>   'Twixt earth and paradise,
> Where things decayed and loved ones lost
>   In dreamy shadows rise,
>
> And, freed from all that's earthly vile,
>   Seem hallowed, pure and bright,
> Like scenes in some enchanted isle
>   All bathed in liquid light.

www.ingramcontent.com/pod-product-compliance
Lightning Source LLC
Chambersburg PA
CBHW030723110426
42739CB00030B/1354

* 9 7 8 3 3 3 7 1 3 6 9 5 6 *